MARIE STOPES

A Checklist of her Writings

MARIE STOPES
A Checklist of her Writings

PETER EATON *and* MARILYN WARNICK

CROOM HELM LONDON

© 1977 Peter Eaton and Marilyn Warnick

Croom Helm Ltd, 2-10 St John's Road, London SW11

ISBN 0-85664-397-1

Printed in Great Britain by
Lowe & Brydone Printers Limited, Thetford, Norfolk

CONTENTS

Sources and Acknowledgements

This checklist is based predominantly on the private collection of Mr Peter Eaton, and on the Stopes' collections of the University of California at Santa Barbara and the University of New York at Stony Brook which were collected and sold by Mr Eaton. We would like to thank the curators of those collections, and also the Librarians of the British Library and the Manchester University Library for their kind assistance. Special acknowledgement is extended to Miss Eve Johansson of the British Library State Paper Room, who located duplicate copies of many catalogued items that were at the bindery, and therefore unavailable for inspection. We would also like to thank the staffs of the Eugenic Society, Fawcett and International Planned Parenthood Libraries for their help and interest.

We are grateful to Mrs Joan Windley of the Marie Stopes Memorial Centre and to Dr Harry and Mrs Mary Stopes-Roe for access to their private collections, and for information unobtainable elsewhere. Dr Stopes-Roe also very kindly provided the photograph used for the frontispiece.

Finally, we would like to thank Mrs Margaret Eaton, Mrs Ruth Hall and Miss Mary Piggott for their patience and advice.

P.E.
M.W.

Part I. Introduction

... Years ago I mapped out a life for myself which I hoped to live, for it seemed an ideal one. I planned to spend twenty years on scientific research, then twenty years on philosophy, and then twenty years in the direct service of humanity, meanwhile writing one poem in which to embody a lifetime's experience of the Universe, and when the poem was finished ... to die! ...

Marie C. Stopes,
In the preface to *Man, Other Poems and a Preface,* 1914.

The above quotation, taken from the preface of Dr Marie Stopes' first published book of poems, tells something about the extraordinary personality of one of the most important women of the twentieth century. At the time that it was written, she was already a distinguished scientist with an international reputation and a long list of scientific publications. Four years later she was to publish *Married Love,* the book that led women out of the sexual repression of the Victorian Age and into sexual awareness. In 1921, she would open the first scientific Birth Control Clinic in the world. She would go on to write books on sex education, health and contraception; plays; poems; a novel; political pamphlets; and hundreds of articles and letters on an incredible variety of topics. She believed that she could contribute something to all the arts and sciences; her contribution to society is unquestionable.

This checklist is a simple list of the writings of Dr Marie Stopes which has been compiled to acquaint the reader with the extent of her interests, and to serve as a preliminary groundwork for a future bibliography. It contains all editions and issues of books, pamphlets, and periodical publications by, or published and edited by, Marie Stopes or by the organisation founded by her, which we have seen, or seen reliably recorded, which were printed in England in her lifetime. It also includes contributions to books and periodicals which have come to our attention, regardless of their place of publication. We have not attempted to list published letters or poetry contributed to periodicals. An asterisk indicates items which we have not personally inspected.

Because Marie Stopes' achievements were in such diverse areas, we have divided her writings into three broad subject fields: SCIENCE; HEALTH AND SOCIAL WELFARE; and LITERATURE AND

TRAVEL. Within each subject field, we have sub-divided the items into the type of publication in which they appear (i.e. books, plays, contributions to periodicals etc.), and then listed them in chronological order from earliest to latest. It is customary in science bibliographies to list entries from the most recent publication back to the earliest. We have not done this in order to preserve consistency throughout the list. The SCIENCE section is therefore presented in chronological order from first to last.

When a title has been published as a portion of a larger work and then as a separate book or pamphlet, it is entered chronologically by the date of its first *separate* publication. Previous appearances are noted with that entry. When there is a possibility of confusion, the item is cross-referenced under the two publication types.

The sections on books and pamphlets provide a minimum of bibliographic description. Books are octavo unless otherwise noted; when known, we have indicated page measurements in centimetres, height first. (When only one measurement is given, it indicates height). We have not described binding varients beyond a mention of material and colour. Lettering on bindings is black unless otherwise noted. All edges are plain and trimmed unless described otherwise. We have mentioned the thousandth of copies printed when it is provided by the publisher on either the title-page or its reverse. Only changes are noted in descriptions of editions and reprints after the first edition entry. Therefore, an item is identical to the one of the same title immediately before it in the list if no changes are given. When known, we have listed the languages into which a book has been translated. Proof copies have been ignored.

Books containing contributions by Dr Stopes are represented only by the first edition in book form. Later impressions are ignored.

The sections on Contributions to Periodicals, particularly in HEALTH AND SOCIAL WELFARE, are very incomplete and can only be considered a rough start towards a comprehensive list. In these sections, we have not confined ourselves to English periodicals. There are some individual items published in other countries which were never, to our knowledge, published in England. In those instances, we have listed both the title and the name of the publication in the original language. Items which have not been personally inspected are included with abridged entries. When a contribution has been reprinted, or when it was circulated as an offprint or extract, we have made a note in square brackets after the regular entry.

For a period during which the editor of *Kingdom Come* was on active service, Marie Stopes had considerable editorial responsibility for it. It has not been established precisely what she contributed to it.

The Sportophyte, a humorous periodical founded and edited by Marie Stopes, has been given a separate heading in the SCIENCE section.

Dr Stopes was the founder of both the Society for Constructive Birth Control and Racial Progress, and the Mothers' Clinic for Constructive

Birth Control. Both of these organisations published pamphlets and hand-
-outs under her direct supervision. Some portions of these publications may
have been written by others, but they were probably written and were
definitely edited by Dr Stopes. We have included them under the Books
and Pamphlets heading of the HEALTH AND SOCIAL WELFARE
section of this checklist.

The Birth Control News, a periodical published by the C B C Society
for over 20 years, is given a separate heading. Occasional individual contributions to the *Birth Control News* by Dr Stopes appeared under her
by-line or under a pseudonym in addition to her unsigned contributions.

We have not made a separate entry for each poem published in a
periodical. Marie Stopes wrote hundreds of poems, many of which were
published in various small literary publications; it would take time dis-
proportionate to their importance to trace them all. The poems that do
appear in the poetry section have been published in collections, or were
separately printed and distributed as single sheet poems. A few poems
with subjects relating to those sections have been listed under SCIENCE
and HEALTH AND SOCIAL WELFARE. Note has been made of
productions of Dr. Stopes' plays when possible. One play, *The Tree of
Desire,* a drama about artificial insemination, was produced at The New
Gateway Theatre, London, in 1955, but was never to our knowledge,
published. There are several other plays mentioned in the Stopes cor-
respondence at the British Library. She wrote 'The New Woman', 'The
Snow Queen', 'Stooping Lady', and a cinema scenario, 'Germany
Miscalculates', in 1915, and then in 1916, a musical comedy 'I told you
so' and a 15th century Italian play 'The Judgement of Borso' (based on
Maurice Hewlett's novel). However, we have found no evidence that any
of these were either produced or published.

Dr Stopes' books and pamphlets were published by a wide variety of
publishers, many of them small and little known. In addition to dis-
seminating articles through her organisations the C B C Society, and the
Mothers' Clinic, she herself published her writings under the name of The
Eclipse Press. During a period in the 40's and 50's she owned and ran the
firm of Alexander Moring Ltd. She very often changed publishers; and
she sometimes changed the title of the item as well. An example of such
changes is *The Study of Plant Life for Young People,* her first book, originally published by Alexander Moring, Ltd., in 1906. The 2nd edition had a
shortened title, *The Study of Plant Life,* and was published by Blackie &
Son Ltd. We have tried to show these changes as clearly as possible.
Married Love was originally banned in the U S We have seen a note in
the Eaton Catalogue of the University of California collection indicating
that the 18th edition was published in the U S under the title of *True
Marriage,* but we have not been able to verify that information by inspection.

We have found six pseudonyms that can be verified as having been
used by Dr Marie Stopes, but there may be others that have escaped our

attention. Dr Stopes often used pseudonyms for her literary pieces in order to avoid the adverse publicity surrounding her birth control and sex education works. She had a sense of humour about them it seems, having once entered a poem in a poetry competition under the name of S. O. Crates!

The Appendix, a list of books and articles about Marie Stopes, includes only items that happened to come to our attention in the course of our research. Some of the articles attack her violently as a threat to decent morals and an evil person preventing the fulfilment of God's wishes; but most hail her as the pioneer of a movement that alleviated the misery of millions of people throughout the world.

Marie Carmichael Stopes was born in Edinburgh on October 15th, 1880, the daughter of a Scotswoman who was a scholar of Shakespeare and his period, and an Englishman who was an engineer and architect, although predominantly interested in archaeology. Her parents kept her away from school until the age of 12; but it soon became apparent that she excelled in science. She entered University College, London, in 1900 and passed the B.Sc. with double honours in Botany and Geology in 1902, after which she was awarded the Gilchrist Studentship for a further year. After this additional year of study and research, she went to Munich to do post-graduate research on cycads. She left Munich with a magna cum laude Ph.D. having survived the *viva voce* examination in German. Upon returning to England, she applied for and won a junior lectureship in botany at Manchester University, becoming the first woman lecturer in the science faculty. During this period she continued her research, published articles, founded the humorous magazine *The Sportophyte,* and found time to join the Tax Resistance League and the Women's Movement. According to Aylmer Maude, her first biographer, it was during this period that her interest in women's problems first began.

In 1905 she obtained the Doctorate of Science, London, becoming the youngest Doctor of Science in England.

Her research continued and her reputation grew. The Royal Society gave her a grant to travel to Japan for a year in order to test a theory she had formed about the existence of certain fossils under particular conditions. She proved herself to be correct, and the year yielded translations of three of the Japanese Nō dramas and a published travel journal, as well as writings about her scientific findings. [The travel journal was reprinted in the U S as recently as 1973.] Upon her return to Manchester she was given the new post of Lecturer in Palaeobotany, and she later held the same post at London University.

In 1910, she was made a Fellow of University College, London. At the age of 30 she was already a distinguished scientist, with a reputation as a leading authority on palaeobotany and coal research.

In 1911, Marie Stopes met her first husband, a Canadian scientist, and they were married shortly afterwards. The unhappy nature of their relationship was the catharsis that turned Marie Stopes' attention from coal and fossils to mankind. For three years she lived with her husband without physical consummation. She went to the British Museum, read all the available books about sex and marriage law, and at the age of 35 in May, 1916, proved in court that her marriage had not been consummated. On these grounds the marriage was annulled in November, 1916, when she was 36, and in order to save other people from the unhappiness she had suffered through a lack of sexual knowledge, Marie Stopes wrote *Married Love, a New Contribution to the Solution of Sex Difficulties.*

The public response to *Married Love* was tremendous. Thousands of letters were addressed to Dr Stopes, and most of them concerned a matter only briefly alluded to on one or two pages of the book – birth control. It was at this point that Dr Stopes and her second husband, Humphrey Verdon Roe, decided to do something to bring birth control to the poor of England. On 17th March 1921, they opened the first scientific birth control clinic in the world, providing free contraceptive advice to any married woman who wanted it. (Through the years Dr Stopes experimented with and adopted various Birth Control methods; and according to the report of the 8th Conference of the International Planned Parenthood Federation of Santiago, Chile, 1967, she experimented with an oral contraceptive, tried out in India, in the last years of her life.)

The rest is well recorded in various histories of the birth control movement and in the writings of Dr Marie Stopes herself. Some opposition came from the medical profession, which objected to Dr Stopes' lack of medical credentials; but most of it came from entrenched beliefs and from the Roman Catholic Church. She fought on and in 1930 the Ministry of Health ceased opposition to her cause in cases where pregnancy would be detrimental to health. A major victory had been won.

Dr Stopes continued to write, but her predominant interest had changed once again, this time from birth control to literature. As she had continued doing some scientific research throughout her Social Welfare decades, she now published an occasional health problem article or pamphlet in between the plays and poetry.

If we had been able to list her published letters, they would have been numbered in hundreds. On topics as varied as longevity, the evolution of spiders, the Catholic Church and litter, Dr Marie Stopes had an opinion; and editors published it. She continued to write almost until her death on October 2nd, 1958.

Marie Stopes, the poet and playwright, has been forgotten; the research of Dr Marie Stopes, the scientist, has served as a stepping stone for later scholars; Dr Marie Stopes, the humane pioneer of the birth control movement in England, has probably done as much as any other single person to ameliorate the human condition.

Part II. Science

ELEMENTARY SCIENCE

1906 THE STUDY OF PLANT LIFE FOR YOUNG PEOPLE

1.	1st edition.	Oct. 1906. London: Alexander Moring, Ltd. The De La More Press. 22 × 14.5 cm. xi + 202 pp., VII plates, illus. Green cloth, pine seedling design on upper cover.
2.	reprint.	Feb. 1907. [designated 2nd impression]
3.	2nd edition.	1910. Re-titled *The Study of Plant Life* for this and subsequent editions. London: Blackie & Son Ltd. xii + 202 pp. + 2 pp. ads., VII plates, illus. Green cloth, leaf skeleton design on upper cover, gilt letters on spine. [Two different paper qualities used throughout].
4.	3rd edition.	1912.
5.	reprint.	1917. no ads. Black letters on spine.
6.	reprint.	1918.
7. *	reprint.	1919.
8.	reprint.	1922.
9. *	reprint.	1924.
10.	reprint.	1927.
11. *	reprint.	1929.
12.	reprint.	1934.

1910 ANCIENT PLANTS. Being a Simple Account of the Past Vegetation of the Earth and of the Recent Important Discoveries Made in This Realm of Nature Study.

13.	1st edition.	1910. London: Blackie & Son, Ltd. 22.3 × 14.5 cm. viii + 198 pp. + 1p. ad., illus., Green cloth, stamped design on upper cover.

1919 BOTANY OR THE MODERN STUDY OF PLANTS.

14.	1st edition.	n.d. The People's Books Series 5. London & Edinburgh: T. C. & E. C. Jack. 16.3 × 10.8 cm. v + 94 pp. + 2 pp. ads., text figs. Green cloth, "The People's Books" emblem and line design on upper cover.

15

15.   2nd edition.   1919. Revised. 15.8 × 10.5 cm. 125 pp. Salmon cloth, 'The People's Books' emblem on upper cover.

BOOKS, PAMPHLETS AND CONTRIBUTIONS TO BOOKS

16.   1904 * SEED-COATS OF CYCADS. [summary of a paper read to the British Association in Cambridge, 1904] London. 1p. [printed by Spottiswoods and Co. Ltd. London].

    1913 THE CRETACEOUS FLORA. PART I – BIBLIOGRAPHY, ALGAE & FUNGI. [from: Catalogue of the Mesozoic Plants in the British Museum (Natural History)].

17.   1st edition.   1913. London: Trustees of the British Museum. 22 × 13.7 cm. xxiii + 281 + 32 pp., 2 plates, 25 texts figs. Brown cloth, gilt letters on spine.

    1914 *THE 'FERN LEDGES'. CARBONIFEROUS FLORA OF ST JOHN, NEW BRUNSWICK.

18.   1st edition.   1914. Ottawa: Geological Survey of Canada: Memoir 41. 8vo. vi + 142 pp., 25 plates, 21 text figs.

    1915 THE CRETACEOUS FLORA. PART II – LOWER GREENSAND (APTIAN) PLANTS OF BRITAIN. [from: Catalogue of the Mesozoic Plants in the British Museum (Natural History)].

19.   1st edition.   1915. London: Trustees of the B. M. 22 × 13.7 cm. xxxvi + 360 pp., 32 plates, 112 text figs. Brown cloth, gilt letters on spine.

    1917 PLANTS AS A SOURCE OF NATIONAL POWER: Chapter 10 in: *The Exploitation of Plants,* edited by F. W. Oliver.

20.   1st edition.   1917. The Imperial Studies Series. London & Toronto: J. M. Dent & Sons, Ltd. 18.6 × 12 cm. pp. 155–170.

    1918 THE CONSTITUTION OF COAL. (With Dr. R. V. Wheeler). Monograph.

21.   1st edition.   1918. London: H. M. Stationery Office for the Department of Scientific and Industrial Research. 8vo. 58 pp., 3 plates.

22. 1922 * THE CONSTITUTION OF COAL, PALAEOBOTANICAL ASPECTS. One chapter in *Coal: A Series of lectures on coal and its utilization.* Sheffield University Dept. of Fuel Technology. London, 1922. 4 to., 41 pp. [see item 72]

CONTRIBUTIONS TO PERIODICALS

23. 1899 SCIENCE CLUB NOTES [by Marie Stopes, Secretary]. In: North London Collegiate School for Girls *Our Magazine.* Ed. by Mrs. Hill. Vol. 24, no. 72, July, 2 pp., Vol. 24, no. 73, Nov., 2 pp.

24. 1903 ON THE LEAF-STRUCTURE OF CORDAITES. *The New Phytologist,* Vol. 2, nos. 4 & 5, April and May. pp. 92–98, plate 9. [reprinted].

25. 1903 THE 'EPIDERMOIDAL' LAYER OF CALAMITE ROOTS. *Annals of Botany,* Sept. pp. 792–794, text figs. 30–32. [offprint].

26. 1903 THE COLONISATION OF A DRIED RIVER BED. (Read before Section K of the British Association at Southport). *The New Phytologist,* Vol. 2, no. 8, Oct. pp. 186–192, 1 text fig.

27. 1904 BEITRAGE ZUR KENNTNIS DER FORTPELANZUNGSORGANE DER CYCADEEN. *Flora Oder Allgemeine Botanische Zeitung,* Vol. 93, Regensburg. pp. 435–482, text figs. 1–37.

28. 1905 ON THE DOUBLE NATURE OF THE CYCADEAN INTEGUMENT. *Annals of Botany,* Vol. 19, no. 76, Oct. pp. 561–566. [reprinted].

29. 1906 THE NUTRITIVE RELATIONS OF THE SURROUNDING TISSUES TO THE ARCHEGONIA IN GYMNOSPERMS. (With Prof. K. Fujii). *Beihefte zum Botanischen Centralblatt,* Vol. 20. 24 pp. plate i. [reprinted].

30. 1906 A NEW FERN FROM THE COAL MEASURES: TUBICAULIS SUTCLIFFIII. 5p Nov. *'Memoirs' and Proceedings of The Manchester Literary and Philosophical Society,* Vol. 50, part 3, no. 10, 34 pp, plates i–iii. [offprint].

31. 1907 * THE RELATION OF THE CONCRETIONARY NODULES OF THE YARRA TO THE CALCAREOUS NODULES KNOWN AS 'COAL-BALLS'. *Geological Magazine,* Decade V, Vol. 4, no. 513, Mar. pp. 106–108. [extract].

32. 1907 THE 'XEROPHYTIC' CHARACTER OF THE GYMNOSPERMS. IS IT AN 'ECOLOGICAL' ADAPTATION? *The New Phytologist,* Vol. 6, no. 2, Feb. pp. 46–50. [reprinted].

33. 1907 A NOTE ON WOUNDED CALAMITES. *Annals of Botany,* Vol. 21, no. 82, Apr. pp. 277–280, plate xxiii, text figs. 1–4. [reprinted].

34. 1907 THE FLORA OF THE INFERIOR OOLITE OF BRORA. *Quarterly Journal Geological Society,* Vol. 63, Aug. pp. 375–382, plate xxvii. [reprinted].

35. 1908 * ON THE PRESENT DISTRIBUTION AND ORIGIN OF THE CALCAREOUS CONCRETIONS IN COAL SEAMS, KNOWN AS 'COAL BALLS'. (With D. M. S. Watson). *Philosophical Transactions of the Royal Society B,* Vol. 200. pp. 167–218, plates xvii–xix.

36. 1909 ON THE TEST-BUILDING HABITS OF THE ANT, LASIUS NIGER NINN, IN JAPAN. [with C. Gordon Hewitt] *'Memoirs' and Proceedings of The Manchester Literary & Philosophical Society,* Vol. 53, Part 3, no. 20. 6 pp., plate i. [reprinted].

37. 1909 PLANT CONTAINING NODULES FROM JAPAN. *Quarterly Journal Geological Society,* Vol. 65, May. pp. 195–205, plate ix.

38. 1909 * EXPEDITION TO THE SOUTHERN COAL MINES. *Fortune,* no. 92, July, pp. 93–107.

39. 1910 * STUDIES ON THE STRUCTURE AND AFFINITIES OF CRETACEOUS PLANTS. (with Prof. K. Fujii). *Philosophical Transactions of the Royal Society B,* Vol. 201. pp. 1–90, plates i–ix.

40.   Abstract. *Annals of Botany,* Vol. 24, no. 93, Jan. 1910. pp. 23–232.

41.   *   *Proceedings of the Royal Society B,* Vol. 81.

42. 1910 THE INTERNAL ANATOMY OF 'NILSSONIA ORIENTALIS'. *Annals of Botany,* Vol. 24, no. 94, Apr. pp. 389–393, plate xxvi, 1 text fig.

43. 1910 THE ANATOMY OF CRETACEOUS PINE LEAVES. (with E. M. Kershaw). *Annals of Botany,* Vol. 24, no. 94, Apr. 1910. pp. 395–402, plates xxvii–xxviii.

44. 1910 ADVENTITIOUS BUDDING AND BRANCHING IN CYCADS. *The New Phytologist,* Vol. 9, nos. 6 & 7, June & July 1910. pp. 235–241, text figs. 8–14. [reprinted].

45. 1910 FURTHER OBSERVATIONS ON THE FOSSIL FLOWER CRETOVARIUM. *Annals of Botany,* Vol. 24, no. 96, Oct. pp. 679–681, plates ivi–ivii.

46. 1910 THE VALUE AND INTEREST OF JAPANESE FOSSILS. *Transactions of the Japan Society,* Vol. 9, pp. 1–12. plates i–iii. [reprinted].

47. 1911 A REPLY TO PROFESSOR JEFFREY'S ARTICLE ON YEZONIA AND CRYPTOMERIOPSIS. *Annals of Botany,* Vol. 25, no. 97, Jan. pp. 269–270.

48. 1911 ON THE TRUE NATURE OF THE CRETACEOUS PLANT OPHIOGLOSSUM GRANULATUM, HEER. *Annals of Botany,* Vol. 25, no. 100, Oct. pp. 903–907, text figs. 1–2.

49. 1911 THE 'DRAGON TREE' OF THE KENTISH RAG. With Remarks on the Treatment of Imperfectly Petrified Woods. *Geological Magazine,* Decade V, Vol. 8, no. 560, Feb. pp. 55–59, 1 text fig. [offprint].

50. 1911 * THE CORRECT NAME FOR THE 'DRAGON TREE' OF THE KENTISH RAG. *Geological Magazine,* Decade V, Vol. 8, no. 568. pp. 467–9.

51. 1912 * PETRIFACTIONS OF THE EARLIEST EUROPEAN ANGIOSPERMS. *Proceedings of the Royal Society B,* Vol. 85. [abstract].

52. * *Transactions of Royal Society B,* Vol. 203, pp. 75–100, plates vi–viii.

53. 1912 * THE RED CRAG PORTRAIT. *Geological Magazine,* Decade V, Vol. 9, Dec. 5. pp. 285–6, text fig. 1.

54. 1912 PALAEOBOTANY VERSUS STRATIGRAPHY IN NEW BRUNSWICK. *British Association Report,* Dundee.

55. 1914 PALAEOBOTANY: ITS PAST AND ITS FUTURE. *Knowledge,* Vol. 37, no. 546, Jan. pp. 15–24, text figs 24–30.

56. 1914 A NEW ARAUCARIOXYLON FROM NEW ZEALAND. (Published by Permission of the Director of the Geological Survey of New Zealand). *Annals of Botany,* Vol. 28, no. 110, Apr. pp. 341–350, plate xx, text figs. 1–3.

57. 1914 A NEW CRETACEOUS PLANT FROM NIGERIA. *Geological Magazine,* Decade VI, Vol. 1, no. 604, pp. 433–5, plate xxxiii, 1 text fig. [extract].

58. 1915 * [SUMMARY OF EXPOSITION OF NEW TYPE OF STEM ANATOMY IN CYCADEODILA] In: Linnean Society of London *Proceedings* – General Meeting, 4th Mar.

59. 1916 * STRUCTURE OF COAL. [essay – review on three memoirs from U S , British and Geological Surveys]. *Science Progress,* July, pp. 73–7.

60. 1916 * [SUMMARY OF A LECTURE GIVEN TO THE GEOLOGICAL SOCIETY OF LONDON, DEC. 20, 1916, ON SOME RECENT RESEARCHES ON MESOZOIC CYCADS] In: *Abstracts of the Proceedings of the Geological Society of London,* no. 998.

61. 1916 AN EARLY TYPE OF THE ABIETINEAE (?) FROM THE CRETACEOUS OF NEW ZEALAND. *Annals of Botany,* Vol. 30, no. 117. pp. 111–125, plate iv, text figs. 1–7. [reprinted].

62. 1916 * COAL, DYES & NATIONAL DEFENSE. *Statist.*

63. 1917 ROOTS IN BENNETTITES. *Annals of Botany,* Vol. 31, no. 122, Apr. pp. 257–259, plate xiv.

64. 1917 * PALAEOBOTANY: BIBLIOGRAPHY. Palaeobotany in 1916, 1917. *Science Progress,* Oct. pp. 229–35.

65. 1918 * PALAEOBOTANY: BIBLIOGRAPHY. *Science Progress.* Oct. pp. 225–32.

66. 1918 * NEW BENNETTITEAN CONES FROM THE BRITISH CRETACEOUS. *Philosophical Transactions of the Royal Society B.* Vol. 208, pp. 389–440, plates xix–xxiv.

67. 1919 * THE FOUR INVISIBLE INGREDIENTS IN BANDED BITUMINOUS COAL: STUDIES IN THE COMPOSITION OF COAL. *Proceedings Royal Society B,* Vol. 90, no. 1. pp. 470–487, plates xi–xii.

68. 1920 * PALAEOBOTANY: BIBLIOGRAPHY – CURRENT. *Science Progress,* pp. 396–8. [abstract].

69. 1920 * BENNETTITES SCOTTI, Sp. Nov., A EUROPEAN PETRIFACTION WITH FOLIAGE. [read 2nd May, 1918]. *Linnean Society's Journal* – *Botany,* Vol. 44, March. pp. 483–496, plates xix–xx, 4 text figs.

70. 1921 * THE MISSING LINKS IN OSMUNDITES. *Annals of Botany,* Vol. 35. pp. 56–61, 1 plate, 1 text fig.

71. 1922 * PALAEOBOTANY: BIBLIOGRAPHY – CURRENT. Apr.

72. 1922 * THE CONSTITUTION OF COAL, PALAEOBOTOANICAL ASPECTS. *Colliery Guardian,* London. 8pp., text figs. [see item 22]

73. 1923 * TERMINOLOGY IN COAL RESEARCH, (with Prof. R. V. Wheeler) 'Fuel', London. pp. 5–9, 1 plate.

74. 1923 * THE SPONTANEOUS COMBUSTION OF COAL. (With Professor R. V. Wheeler). Bulletin No. 1 of 'Fuel'. In: *Colliery Guardian*, London. 125 pp., 2 plates, text figs.

75. 1923 * CONTRIBUTION PALÉOBOTANIQUE À LA CONNAISSANCE DU CHARBON. Résumé of Communication to the Congress in Paris. In: *Chaleur et Industrie*, Paris.

76. 1926 * CRYSTALLINE NATURE OF THE CHIEF CONSTITUENTS OF ORDINARY COAL. (With Cyril S. Fox). *Nature*, Dec. 25.

77. 1931 THE PEA. A poem. *Armchair Science*, monthly, Vol. 11, no. 11, Feb. p. 639. [Originally appeared in Vol. IV, 1913 of *The Sportophyte*, see item 81]

78. 1935 * ON THE PETROLOGY OF BANDED BITUMINOUS COAL. *Fuel in Science and Practive*, Jan.

79. 1953 * 'THE DISCOVERY', PART 1 of 3 in: A DISCOVERY OF HUMAN SKULLS WITH STONE ARTIFACTS AND ANIMAL BONES IN A FISSURE AT PORTLAND. By M.C. Stopes, K. P. Oakley, and L. H. Wells. *Proceedings of the Dorset Natural History and Archaeological Society for 1952*, Vol. 74. pp. 39–47, 1 plate, 2 text figs. [reprinted].

80. 1955 THE NEW BRITISH MUSEUM LAW. *Nature*, Vol. 175, May 21. 3 pp. [reprinted].

THE SPORTOPHYTE

81. 1910 THE SPORTOPHYTE. A British Journal of Botanical Humour. Founded and Edited by Marie C. Stopes, Palaeophytologist.
Vol. I, Apr., 1910. Manchester. 8 vo. 23 pp. Orange paper covers.
Vol. II, Apr., 1911. London. 24 pp.
Vol. III, Apr., 1912.
Vol. IV, Apr., 1913. Sub-title changed to 'The Humorous Botanical Annual'.

Part III. Health and Social Welfare

BOOKS AND PAMPHLETS

1918   MARRIED LOVE. A New Contribution to the Solution of Sex Difficulties. With a Preface by Dr Jessie Murray and Letters from Professor E. H. Starling, F R S , and Father Stanislaus St. John, S.J.

82.	1st edition.	[Mar. 26, 1918.] London: A. C. Fifield. 18.5 × 12 cm. xvii + 116 pp. Maroon cloth, gilt letters on spine.
83.	2nd edition.	May 17, 1918.
84.	3rd edition.	June 25, 1918.
85.	4th edition.	Aug. 2, 1918. Completing 10,000 copies. xvii + 116 pp. + 1p. ad.
86.	reprint.	Aug. 7, 1918. Completing 11,000.
87.	reprint.	Sept. 1918. Completing 12,000.
88.	5th edition.	Sept. 19, 1918. Completing 17,000.
89.	6th edition.	Feb. 3, 1919. Enlarged. xvii + 123 pp. + 1p. ad.
90.	7th edition.	May 29, 1919. Letter from Father Stanislaus St. John deleted. S. J., Revised and enlarged. London: G. P. Putnam's Sons, Ltd., 189 pp. + 1p. ad.
91.	reprint.	Aug. 14, 1919.
92.	reprint.	Jan. 1, 1920.
93.	8th edition.	May 10, 1920.
94.	9th edition.	July 19, 1920. Revised.
95.	reprint.	Jan. 19, 1921.
96.	reprint.	Mar. 19, 1921. Completing 116,000.
97.	reprint.	May 19, 1921. Completing 126,000.
98.	reprint.	July 29, 1921. Completing 141,000.
99.	reprint.	Oct. 29, 1921. Completing 161,000.
100.	reprint.	Mar. 9, 1922. Completing 166,000.
101.	* reprint.	May 9, 1922.
102.	10th edition.	June 9, 1922. Revised. Completing 181,000. 191 pp. + 1p. ad.
103.	reprint.	Sept. 9, 1922. Completing 191,000.
104.	* reprint.	Nov. 29, 1922.
105.	11th edition.	Mar. 9, 1923. Revised. Completing 211,000. 191 pp. + 4 pp. ads.

106.		reprint.	Mar. 19, 1923. Completing 221,000.
107.		reprint.	Mar. 20, 1923.
108.	*	reprint.	Mar. 21, 1923.
109.		reprint.	Mar. 23, 1923. Completing 251,000.
110.		reprint.	Mar. 24, 1923. Completing 261,000.
111.	12th edition.		Mar. 1923. Revised. Completing 281,000. 190 pp. + 4 pp. ads.
112.		reprint.	Mar. 1923. Completing 291,000.
113.	*	reprint.	Mar. 1923.
114.	*	reprint.	Apr., 1923.
115.		reprint.	Apr., 1923. Completing 306,000.
116.		reprint.	May, 1923. Overseas Edition. Completing 311,000.
117.	*	reprint.	May, 1923.
118.	*	reprint.	June, 1923.
119.	*	reprint.	June, 1923.
120.		reprint.	July, 1923. Completing 365,000.
121.	*	reprint.	Aug., 1923.
122.		reprint.	Sept. 1923. Completing 371,000.
123.	* 13th edition.		Oct. 1923.
124.	14th edition.		Oct. 1923. Revised. Completing 396,000. xxi pp. + 169 pp. + 5 pp. ads.
125.		reprint.	Sept. 1923. Completing 405,000.
126.		reprint.	Dec. 1923. Overseas Edition. Completing 406,000.
127.		reprint.	Jan. 1924. Completing 416,000.
128.		reprint.	May, 1924. Completing 436,000.
129.	15th edition.		n.d. London: G. P. Putnam's Sons. [limited to 450 copies signed by the Author]. 23 × 15.3 cm. Photo of Stopes on frontis, xxi + 169 pp. Grey cloth, gilt tooling on spine. Edges gilt topped, uncut.
130.	16th edition.		Aug., 1924. Revised. Completing 446,500. xxi + 169 pp. + 4 pp. ads. Binding as 14th ed.
131.		reprint.	Oct., 1924. Completing 456,500.
132.		reprint.	Nov., 1924. Completing 466,500.
133.	*	reprint.	Jan., 1925.
134.	*	reprint.	Apr., 1925.
135.	*	reprint.	May, 1925.
136.		reprint.	June, 1925. Completing 501,500.
137.	17th edition.		Mar., 1926. Completing 540,500. xxi + 169 pp. + 5 pp. ads.
138.	*	reprint.	Apr., 1926.
139.		reprint.	June, 1926. Completing 545,500.
140.	18th edition.		Aug., 1926. Completing 565,500. xxi +

		163 pp. + 5 pp. ads.
141.	* reprint.	Feb., 1926.
142.	reprint.	Mar., 1926. Completing 583,500.
143.	* reprint.	June, 1927.
144.	reprint.	Sept., 1927. Completing 610,000.
145.	* reprint.	Apr., 1928.
146.	reprint.	July, 1928. Completing 630,000.
147.	reprint.	Aug., 1928. Overseas edition. Completing 640,000. 18.5 × 12 cm. Grey wrappers, green letters.
148.	* reprint.	Jan., 1929.
149.	reprint.	Mar., 1929.
150.	reprint.	Aug., 1929. Completing 675,000. xxi + 163 pp. + 6 pp. ads.
151.	* reprint.	Nov., 1929.
152.	reprint.	Feb., 1930. Completing 690,000.
153.	19th edition.	July, 1930. Completing 700,000. xxi + 170 pp. + 6 pp. ads.
154.	reprint.	Mar., 1931. Completing 710,000.
155.	20th edition.	
156.	reprint.	Aug., 1931. Completing 720,000.
157.	reprint.	Nov., 1931. Completing 725,000.
158.	reprint.	Aug., 1932. Completing 735,000.
159.	reprint.	Nov., 1932. Completing 740,000.
160.	reprint.	Feb., 1933. Completing 745,000.
161.	21st edition.	Aug., 1933. Completing 750,000. xxi + 172 pp. + 6 pp. ads.
162.	reprint.	Nov., 1933. Completing 755,000.
163.	reprint.	Apr., 1934. Completing 765,000.
164.	* reprint.	July, 1934.
165.	reprint.	Nov., 1934.
166.	* reprint.	Mar., 1935.
167.	reprint.	July 1935. Completing 780,000.
168.	22nd edition.	Dec., 1935. Completing 785,000. xxi + 170 pp. + 8 pp. ads.
170.	reprint.	Aug., 1937. Completing 805,000.
171.	reprint.	Jan., 1938. Completing 810,000.
172.	reprint.	Jan., 1939. Completing 825,000.
173.	reprint.	May, 1939. Completing 830,000.
174.	24th edition.	Oct., 1940. Completing 855,000. 18.3 × 11.5 cm. Red cloth.
175.	* reprint.	June, 1941.
176.	reprint.	Sept., 1941. Completing 870,000. Maroon cloth.
177.	reprint.	Mar., 1942. Completing 875,000. Only 2 pp. ads.

178.		reprint.	June, 1942. Completing 880,000. 8 pp. ads.
179.	*	reprint.	Oct., 1942.
180.		reprint.	Jan., 1943. Completing 890,000. Red cloth.
181.	*	reprint.	Completing 895,000.
182.	*	reprint.	
183.	*	reprint.	n.d. Completing 910,000. Overseas edition. Blue paper, maroon letters.
184.	*	reprint.	maroon cloth.
185.	*	reprint.	Completing 930,000.
186.	*	reprint.	Completing 935,000. Red cloth.
187.		25th edition.	
188.		26th edition.	July, 1952. Completing 1,020,000. London: Hogarth Press. 18.5 × 12 cm. xviii + 151 pp. + 2 pp. ads. Dark pink cloth.
189.	*	27th edition.	
190.		28th edition.	Aug., 1955. Completing 1,032,250. xviii + 155 pp + 2 pp. ads.

Translations: Afrikaans, Arabic, Chinese, Czech, Danish, Norweigian, Dutch, German, Hungarian, Hindi, Italian, Roumanian, Spanish and Swedish.
English editions: Australia, Canada, India, the USA, and in Braille.

1918		WISE PARENTHOOD. A Sequel to *Married Love*. A Book for Married People. With an introduction by Arnold Bennett.
191.	1st edition.	Nov. 18, 1918. London: A. C. Fifield. 19 × 12.8 cm. viii + 34 pp. Brown wrappers, red and white label.
192.	2nd edition.	Jan. 1, 1919.
193.	3rd edition.	Mar. 20, 1919.
194.	4th edition.	Apr. 22, 1919.
195.	5th edition.	Aug. 19, 1919. Revised and enlarged. London: G. P. Putnam's Sons, Ltd. 19 × 12.6 cm. 60 pp. + 4 pp. ads. Maroon cloth, gilt letters on spine.
196. *	reprint.	Jan. 1, 1920.
197.	6th edition.	July 9, 1920. Revised and enlarged. ix + 55 pp. + 6 pp. ads. Brown cloth, Green letters on spine.
198.	reprint.	Feb. 9, 1921. [Erroneously designated 7th edition].

199.		reprint.	May 2, 1921. Completing 96,000. Gilt letters on spine.
200.		7th edition.	June 9, 1921. [some copies are erroneously dated Feb. 9, 1921]. ix + 55 pp. + 5 pp. ads. + 10 pp. 'History of the Clinic'.
201.		reprint.	Nov. 9, 1921.
202.		8th edition.	May 9, 1922. Revised and enlarged. Completing 160,000. xi + 58 pp. + 8 pp. ads.
203.		9th edition.	Sept. 9, 1922. Revised and enlarged. Completing 165,000. xii + 64 pp. + 9 pp. ads.
204.		10th edition.	Dec. 9, 1922. Revised and enlarged. Completing 170,000. [xii + 64 pp + 9 pp. ads].
205.		reprint.	Feb. 19, 1923. Completing 175,000.
206.		reprint.	Feb. 26, 1923. Completing 185,000.
207.		reprint.	Feb. 27, 1923. Completing 195,000.
208.		11th edition.	Mar. 9, 1923. Revised and enlarged. Completing 205,000. xii + 62 pp. + 9 pp. ads.
209.	*	reprint.	Mar., 1923. Completing 215,000.
210.		reprint.	Apr., 1923. Completing 225,000.
211.		reprint.	Apr., 1923. Completing 235,000.
212.		reprint.	May, 1923, Completing 245,000.
213.		reprint.	June, 1923. Completing 255,000.
214.	*	reprint.	July, 1923.
215.	*	reprint.	Aug., 1923.
216.		reprint.	Aug., 1923. Completing 285,000.
217.		12th edition.	Oct., 1923. Revised and enlarged. Completing 295,000. xii + 62 pp. + 13 pp. ads.
218.		reprint.	Nov., 1923. Completing 305,000.
219.	*	reprint.	Feb., 1924.
220.		reprint.	Apr., 1924. Completing 325,000.
221.		reprint.	Apr., 1924. Completing 325,000.
222.		reprint.	June, 1924. Completing 335,000.
223.		reprint.	Aug., 1924. Completing 345,000.
224.		reprint.	Sept., 1924. Completing 355,000.
225.		reprint.	Nov., 1924. Completing 365,000.
226.		reprint.	Jan., 1925. Completing 375,000.
227.		reprint.	Apr., 1925. Completing 385,000.
228.	*	reprint.	June 1925.

229.		reprint.	Sept., 1925. Completing 405,000.
230.		reprint.	Nov., 1925. Completing 415,000.
231.		reprint.	Apr., 1925. Completing 425,000.
232.	*	reprint.	July, 1926.
233.	*	reprint.	Sept., 1926.
234.		reprint.	Jan., 1927. Completing 455,000.
235.	* 13th edition.		Mar., 1927.
236.	14th edition.		Aug., 1927. Revised and enlarged. Completing 476,000. xiv + 68 pp. + 11 pp. ads.
237.	15th edition.		Feb., 1928. Completing 486,000. xix + 81 pp. + 3 pp. recommended reading list + 10 pp. ads.
238.		reprint.	May, 1928. Completing 496,000.
239.		reprint.	Oct., 1928. Completing 506,000.
240.		reprint.	Jan., 1929. Completing 516,000.
241.		reprint.	June, 1929. Completing 526,000.
242.	*	reprint.	Sept., 1929.
243.	16th edition.		Apr., 1930. Revised. Completing 451,000.
244.		reprint.	July, 1930. Completing 551,000.
245.		reprint.	Jan., 1931.
246.	17th edition.		May, 1931. Revised. Completing 561,000. xix + 88 pp. + 3 pp. recommended reading list + 10 pp. ads.
247.		reprint.	Aug., 1931. Completing 566,000.
248.	18th edition.		Jan., 1932. Revised. Completing 571,000.
249.		reprint.	June, 1932. Completing 576,000.
250.	*	reprint.	Sept., 1932.
251.		reprint.	Feb., 1933. Completing 586,000.
252.		reprint.	Aug., 1933. Completing 591,000.
253.		reprint.	Feb., 1934. Completing 596,000.
254.	*	reprint.	
255.	19th edition.		Apr., 1935. Revised.
256.		reprint.	Sept., 1935. Completing 611,000.
257.	20th edition.		Aug., 1936. Revised. Completing 616,000. xvii + 95 pp. + 3 pp. reading list + 10 pp. ads.
258.	*	reprint.	Mar., 1937.
259.	21st edition.		Nov., 1937. Revised. Completing 626,000. xx + 95 pp. + 3 pp. reading list + 10 pp. ads.
260.	22nd edition.		Oct., 1938. Revised. Completing 631,000.
261.	*	reprint.	Aug., 1939.
262.	23rd edition.		July, 1940. Revised. Completing 641,000. [some reprints are bound in red cloth rather than the usual maroon].

263.	*	reprint.	July, 1941.
264.		reprint.	Feb., 1942. Completing 661,000.
265.	*	reprint.	June, 1942.
266.		reprint.	Completing 666,000.
267.	*	reprint.	
268.		reprint.	Completing 676,000.
269.		reprint.	Completing 681,000.
270.	*	reprint.	
271.		24th edition.	June, 1947. Revised. Completing 696,000. 1 ad. dropped.
272.		25th edition.	Sept., 1951. Completing 706,000. Sub-title changed to 'A Treatise on Birth Control For Married People'. xx + 98 pp. + 3 pp. reading list + 7 pp. ads.

Translations: Afrikaans, Chinese, Danish, Norwegian, Czech, Dutch, German, Hindi, Hungarian, Portuguese, Spanish, Swedish.

1919 A LETTER TO WORKING MOTHERS. On How To Have Healthy Children and Avoid Weakening Pregnancies.

273.		1st edition.	Apr., 1919. Leatherhead: the Author. 15 pp.
274.	*	2nd edition.	Feb., 1923. London: Mother's Clinic. 18.3 × 12 cm. 15 pp. Green wrappers.
275.	*	reprint.	Sept., 1923.
276.	*	reprint.	Nov., 1923.
277.	*	reprint.	Feb., 1923.
278.	*	reprint.	June, 1924.
279.	*	reprint.	Oct., 1924.
280.	*	3rd edition.	Jan., 1925.
281.	*	reprint.	Mar., 1925.
282.	*	reprint.	June, 1925.
283.		reprint.	Aug., 1925.
284.	*	reprint.	Oct., 1925.
285.		reprint.	Oct., 1925.
286.	*	reprint.	Nov., 1925.
287.		reprint.	Jan., 1926.
288.		4th edition.	Mar., 1926. 16 pp.
289.		5th edition.	Apr., 1926.
290.		reprint.	Sept., 1926.
291.		6th edition.	Dec., 1926.
292.		reprint.	May, 1927.
293.		reprint.	

294.	*	reprint.	
295.	*	reprint.	
296.		reprint.	May, 1928.
297.		7th edition.	Apr., 1929.
298.	*	reprint.	June, 1929.
299.		8th edition.	Nov., 1929.
300.	*	9th edition.	Mar., 1931.
301.	*	reprint.	Aug., 1931.
302.		10th edition.	June, 1934. 18 pp.
303.		11th edition.	Apr., 1935.
304.		12th edition.	Nov., 1935.
305.		13th edition.	June, 1941.
306.		14th edition.	Sept., 1943.
307.		15th edition.	1947. Retitled *Practical Birth Control or How to Have Healthy Children and Avoid Weakening Pregnancies.* London: Mothers' Clinic. 18.3 × 12.5 cm. 20 pp. Green wrappers.

1920   RADIANT MOTHERHOOD. A Book for Those Who are Creating the Future.

308.	1st edition.	Aug., 9, 1920. London: G. P. Putnam's Sons, Ltd., 18.7 × 12.5 cm. 246 pp. + 9 pp. ads. Maroon cloth, gilt letters on spine.
309.	reprint.	Aug., 19, 1920.
310.	reprint.	Sept., 17, 1920. viii + 236 pp. + 9 pp. ads.
311.	reprint.	Dec., 29, 1920.
312.	reprint.	Sept., 9, 1921.
313.	reprint.	Apr., 29, 1922.
314.	2nd edition.	Nov., 9, 1922.
315.	reprint.	Mar., 9, 1923.
316.	3rd edition.	Oct., 9, 1923.
317.	reprint.	Apr., 1924.
318.	* reprint.	
319.	4th edition.	Nov., 1925.
320.	reprint.	Oct., 1926.
321.	reprint.	Oct., 1927.
322.	reprint.	June, 1929.
323.	5th edition.	Mar., 1931. x + 202 pp. + 6 pp. ads.
324.	6th edition.	Aug., 1934.
325.	reprint.	May, 1935.
326.	reprint.	Nov., 1935.
327.	7th edition.	Nov., 1938. Sub-title changed to: 'A Book for Pregnant Women and their Husbands'. x + 203 pp. + 6 pp. ads.
328.	8th edition.	Jan. 1940. x + 204 pp. + 6 pp. ads.
329.	reprint.	Sept., 1941.

330.   reprint.   Dec., 1943.
331.   reprint.   Apr., 1946. x + 204 pp. + 7 pp. ads. Red
                         cloth.
332.   9th edition.   Jan. 1948. 212 pp.

         Translations: Czech, Danish, Norwegian, German, Dutch,
         Hungarian, Portuguese and Spanish.

[1920]* BABIES AND UNREST.

333.   1st edition.   [1920]. New York: Voluntary Parenthood
                            League. 7 pp.
334. 1920   A NEW GOSPEL. A Revelation of God Uniting
            Physiology and the Religions of Man. Putnam's. 17.5 ×
            12.3 cm. 15 pp. Green paper covers.

     1921   QUEEN'S HALL MEETING ON CONSTRUC-
            TIVE BIRTH CONTROL. Speeches and impressions.

335.   *   1st edition.   July, 1921. London: G. P. Putnam's Sons.
                            47 pp. 18.4 × 12.4 cm. Blue wrappers.
336.   reprint.   Apr., 1923.

     1921   THE SOCIETY FOR CONSTRUCTIVE BIRTH
            CONTROL AND RACIAL PROGRESS. RECORD
            OF INAUGURAL MEETING, Aug. 16, 1921.

337.   1st edition.   London: C. B. C. Society. 25.5 × 20.5 cm.
                            3pp.

     1921 *THE MOTHERS' CLINIC FOR BIRTH CON-
            TROL. [Descriptive pamphlet].

338.   1st edition.   1921. London: Mothers' Clinic. 10 pp.
339.   another ed.   1921. 12 pp.
                            [there are probably other un-recorded
                            editions].

     1921   WHAT IS CONSTRUCTIVE BIRTH CONTROL?
            WHO SHOULD JOIN THE C.B.C.?

340.   1st edition.   1921. London: C.B.C. Society. 1 sheet.
341.   4 other ed.   1924–1935.

     1921   CONSTITUTION, OFFICERS AND MEMBER-
            SHIP FORM OF THE SOCIETY FOR CON-
            STRUCTIVE BIRTH CONTROL.

342.   9 editions.   [1921–1955]. London: C.B.C. Society.

     1921   MANIFESTO OF THE 'C B C' – BABIES IN THE
            RIGHT PLACE.

| 343. | 1st edition. | Oct., 1921. London: C.B.C. Society. 1 sheet. |
| 344. | 2nd edition. | |

1921 TRUTH ABOUT VENEREAL DISEASE.

345.	1st edition.	Jan., 1921. London: Putnam's 19 × 12.7 cm. 52 pp. Grey wrappers and also brown cloth.
346.	reprint.	Feb., 1921.
347.	reprint.	May, 1921.
348.	reprint.	July, 1921.
349.	reprint.	July, 1923.
350.	2nd edition.	Aug., 1925. Revised. London: Putnam's. 60 pp. + 4 pp. ads. Maroon cloth.
351.	reprint.	May, 1927.
352.	reprint.	Dec., 1928.
353.	reprint.	May, 1930.
354.	reprint.	Apr., 1934.
355.	3rd edition.	Oct., 1939. Retitled 'Prevention of Venereal Disease' for this and subsequent editions. Thoroughly revised and enlarged. London: Putnam's. 62 pp. Brown paper covered boards.
356.	reprinted.	12 times.

1921 VERBATIM REPORT OF THE TOWN HALL MEETING.

| 357. | 1st edition. | Oct. 27, 1921. N.Y.: Voluntary Parenthood League. 23 × 15.7 cm. 23 pp. + 1p. ad. Grey wrappers. |

EARLY DAYS OF BIRTH CONTROL.

| 358. | 1st edition. | Apr., 1922. London: Putnam's. 18.7 × 12.7 cm. 32 pp. Grey wrappers, blue letters. |
| 359. | 2nd edition. | May, 1922. |

1922 A NEW GOSPEL TO ALL PEOPLES. A Revelation of God Uniting Physiology and the Religions of Man.

360.	* Privately printed	June, 1920. 14 pp.
361.	1st edition.	Jan., 1922. London: Arthur L. Humphreys. 18.9 × 13.5 cm. 27 pp. Cream paper covered boards, blue letters.
362.	2nd edition.	Mar., 1922. London: The Mothers' C.B.C. Clinic. 18.6 × 13.5 cm.

363.	1st edition.	Dec., 1922. London: Putnam. 16.8 × 10.7 cm. 25 pp. + 3 pp. ads. Blue wrappers, navy letters, gilt border. [One of the 14 chapters in 'Radiant Motherhood' where it is entitled 'The Weakest Link in the Human Chain'. [See item 308]
364.	reprint.	Apr., 1923.
365.	reprint.	Apr., 1924.
366.	* reprint.	Sept., 1925.
367.	* reprint.	July, 1928.
368.	reprint.	Oct., 1933.
369.	* reprint.	July, 1935.
370.	* reprint.	July, 1937.
371.	* reprint.	Apr., 1939.
372.	reprint.	June, 1942.
373.	* reprint.	Feb., 1944.
374.	* reprint.	June, 1945.
375.	reprint.	Aug., 1946.

1923 CONTRACEPTION (Birth Control). Its Theory, History And Practice.
A Manual for The Medical and Legal Professions. With an Introduction by Prof. Sir William Bayliss, M.A., D.Sc., F.R.S., and Introductory Notes by Sir James Barr, M.D., L.L.D., F.R.C.P., Dr. C. Rolleston, Dr. Jane Hawthorne and Obscurus.

376.	1st edition.	June 27, 1923. London: John Bale, Sons & Danielsson Ltd. 21.3 × 13.3 cm. xxiii + 418 pp. IV plates. Fern green cloth, stamped, gilt letters.
377.	reprint.	Dec., 1923.
378.	reprint.	July, 1924.
379.	reprint.	July, 1925. xxiii + 418 pp. + 2 pp. ads., IV plates.
380.	reprint.	Mar., 1926.
381.	2nd edition.	June, 1927. New and Enlarged. Completing 40,000. xxvi + 480 pp., V plates.
382.	reprint.	Jan., 1928.
383.	reprint.	Sept., 1929.
384.	3rd edition.	July, 1931. New and Enlarged edition. Notes by Obscurus deleted. London: G. P. Putnam's Sons. xxvii + 487 pp., X plates. Brown cloth.
385.	reprint.	June, 1932.

386.		4th edition.	May, 1934. Revised and enlarged. xxvii + 487 pp., X plates.
387.		reprint.	Nov., 1935.
388.		reprint.	Oct., 1937.
389.		5th edition.	Aug., 1941. Revised and enlarged. xxvii + 491 pp., X plates.
390.		6th edition.	Oct., 1946. Revised and enlarged.
391.		7th edition.	June, 1949. No lettering on upper cover.
392.		8th edition.	Mar., 1952. xx + 507 pp., X plates. Blue cloth.

1923 THE TENETS OF THE C.B.C.

| 393. | | 1st edition. | Mar., 1923. London: C.B.C. Society. 20 x 12.5 cm. 4 pp. [there are several other editions not seen by the compiler of this list]. |

394. 1924 ADVANTAGES OF JOINING THE C.B.C. London: C.B.C. Society. 1 sheet.

395. 1925 * VERBATIM REPORT OF THE TOWN HALL MEETING. (contains verbatim report of Stopes' speech). New York: Voluntary Parenthood League. 25 pp.

1925 THE FIRST FIVE THOUSAND. Being The First Report of the First Birth Control Clinic in the British Empire, 'The Mothers' Clinic' For Constructive Birth Control at 61, Marlborough Road, Holloway, London N.19.

| 396. | | 1st edition. | Feb. 18, 1925. London: John Bale, Sons & Danielsson, Ltd. 18 x 11.6 cm. 67 pp. + 3 pp. ads. Light blue cloth, gilt letters on upper cover. |

1926 BIBLIOGRAPHY. (46) BIRTH CONTROL AND POPULATION PROBLEMS. A Selected List of books suitable for general readers.

397.	*	1st edition.	July, 1926. London: C.B.C. Society. 1 sheet.
398.	*	2nd edition.	Mar., 1927. Revised.
399.	*	3rd edition.	
400.	*	4th edition.	1934. 3pp.
401.	*	5th edition.	1940.

1926 THE HUMAN BODY AND ITS FUNCTIONS

| 402. | | 1st edition. | Mar. 3, 1926. London: The Gill Publishing Co. Ltd. 20.2 x 14.2 cm. 224 pp. 53 text figs., VII colour plates. Dark green cloth, gilt letters on spine. |

403.	reissued.	Jan., 1929. [cheap edition] London: G. P. Putnam's Sons. 20 × 14 cm. Maroon cloth, gilt letters on spine.
404.	reprint.	Dec., 1929.
405.	reprint.	Nov., 1930.
406.	reprint.	Jan., 1932.
407.	reprint.	Oct., 1932.
408.	reprint.	Mar., 1934.
409.	reprint.	Jan., 1937.
410.	reprint.	Jan., 1940.

1926 SEX AND THE YOUNG

| 411. | 1st edition. | 1926. London: The Gill Publishing Co. Ltd. 20.5 × 14 cm. v + 1 blank + 190 pp. + 4 pp. ads. Blue cloth, stamped, gilt letters on spine. |
| 412. | 2nd edition. | 1929. Reissued. London: G. P. Putnam's Sons. 20 × 14½ cm. Binding: Maroon cloth, gilt letters on spine. [2 different printers]. |

1928 ENDURING PASSION. Further New Contributions to the Solution of Sex Difficulties being the continuation of *Married Love.*

413.		1st edition.	Oct. 18, 1928. London: G. P. Putnam's Sons. 18.1 × 12 cm. xiv + 214 pp. + 6pp. ads. Maroon cloth, gilt letters on spine.
414.	*	reprint.	
415.		2nd edition.	Feb., 1929. Revised and including all prescriptions. 18.4 × 12 cm. xiv + 216 pp. + 6 pp. ads.
416.		reprint.	Aug., 1929.
417.		reprint.	Sept., 1929.
418.	*	3rd edition.	Sept., 1930.
419.		4th edition.	May, 1931. xiv + 220 pp. + 6 pp. ads.
420.	*	reprint.	Sept., 1932.
421.		5th edition.	Apr., 1934.
422.		reprint.	Nov., 1934.
423.		reprint.	July, 1935.
424.		6th edition.	Aug., 1936. xvi + 220 pp. + 8 pp. ads. Bindings vary from maroon to red cloth; some copies are printed on very thin paper.
425.		reprint.	May, 1937.
426.		reprint.	Apr., 1938.
427.		reprint.	Apr., 1938.
428.		reprint.	Jan., 1939.

429.	reprint.	Oct., 1939.
430.	reprint.	July, 1940.
431.	reprint.	Sept., 1941.
432.	reprint.	Oct., 1942.
433.	reprint.	Apr., 1944.
434.	reprint.	Aug., 1945.
435.	reprint.	Oct., 1946.
436.	reprint.	Mar., 1948.
437.	7th edition.	May, 1953. London: The Hogarth Press. 18.5 × 12. 3 cm. xii + 159 pp. + 5 pp. ads. Jade Green cloth, gilt letters on spine. [Dedication changed].
438.	8th edition.	Jan., 1956.

Translations: Dutch, Danish, German, Norwegian, Finish, Spanish, Swedish, Gujarati, Afrikaans.

1929 SEX AND RELIGION.

	1st published.	1926. 1 chapter in *Sex and the Young.* [see item 411].
439.	1st edition.	Dec., 1929. London: Putnam's. 16.5 × 10.5 cm. 30 pp. Brown wrappers.
440.	reprint.	Mar., 1936.
441.	reprint.	Nov., 1946. 24 pp. Blue wrappers, navy letters.

1929 MOTHER ENGLAND. A Contemporary History self-written by those who have had no historian.

| 442. | 1st edition. | Dec., 1929. London: John Bale Sons & Danielsson, Ltd. 21.3 × 13.3 cm. vi + 206 pp. Blue cloth, gilt design and letters. |
| 443. | 2nd edition. | May, 1930. |

[1930?] THE SECRET ENEMY . . . FOR PARENTS. Practical Pamphlets on Important subjects.

| 444. | 1st edition. | [1930?]. London: The Mothers' Clinic Ltd. 11.4 ×9 cm. 15 pp. Pale blue wrappers, white label. |

1930 *C.B.C. BULLETIN NO. 1*
PRELIMINARY NOTES ON VARIOUS TECHNICAL ASPECTS OF THE CONTROL OF CONCEPTION Based on the ANALYSED DATA from TEN THOUSAND CASES attending the Pioneer Mothers' Clinic London.

| 445. | 1st edition. | Mar., 1930. London: Mothers' Clinic. 21.5 × 13.8 cm. 44 pp. + 1p. C.B.C. Society & |

Clinic Subscription form. Blue covers,
wrappers, title cover.

446. reprint. July, 1933. 52 pp. + C.B.C. Soc. & Clinic Subscription form. [pp. 49–52 – A Few of the Things We Have Done].

1930 *C.B.C. BULLETIN NO. 2*
COITAL INTERLOCKING. A Physiological Discovery.

447. 1st edition. July, 1930. London: Mothers' Clinic. 21.5 × 13.8 cm. 6 pp. pamphlet. Green title cover.

448. reprint. 1952. 8 pp.

1930 A FEW OF THE THINGS WE HAVE DONE

449. 1st edition. 1930. London: C.B.C. Society. 1 sheet.
450. another ed. 1932.

1931 SOME OBJECTION TO CONTRACEPTION ANSWERED.

1st published. June, 1923. As Chapter VIII in 1st and 2nd editions of *Contraception, its Theory, History and Practice.* [see items 376–383. Dropped from 3rd edition, 1931.]

451. 1st separate publication. Oct., 1931. Limited. London: John Bale, Sons & Danielsson.

1933 ROMAN CATHOLIC METHODS OF BIRTH CONTROL. With an Intro. by: The Rev. Percy Dearmer, D.D., Prefatory Notes by: Hugh Walpole, Julian Huxley, Lady Acland, Sir W. Arbuthnot Lane, Bart.

452. 1st edition. June 1933. London: Peter Davies. 18.3 × 12.3 cm. xv + 235 pp. Red cloth, gilt letters.

453. reprint. 1945.
454. reprint. 1949.

1934 *C.B.C. BULLETIN No. 3*
EQUIPPING A BIRTH CONTROL CLINIC. [Based largely on Chapter XV in the book *Contraception . . .*, 3rd ed.]

455. 1st edition. 1934. London: Mothers' Clinic. 21.5 × 13.8 cm. 15 pp. pamphlet. title cover.

456. 2nd edition. 1952.

		1934	BIRTH CONTROL TODAY. A Practical Handbook For Those Who Want To Be Their Own Masters In This Vital Matter.

457.   1st edition.   July 18, 1934. Pocket size, illustrated. London: John Bale, Sons & Danielsson, Ltd. 16.2 × 10.3 cm. 237 pp. + 8 pp. ads. Blue cloth, stamped gilt.

458.   2nd edition.   Oct., 1934.

459. * 3rd edition.   Sept., 1935.

460. * 4th edition.   June, 1939.

461. * 5th edition.   June, 1939.

462. * 6th edition.   Oct., 1940.

463. * 7th edition.   Sept., 1941.

464. *   reprint.   1945.

465. * 8th edition.   1947.

466.   9th edition.   1948. Pocket size, illus. London: Alex Moring Ltd. 16 × 10.8 cm. 242 pp. + 6 pp. ads. Red cloth.

467.   10th edition.   1953. Revised and brought up to date. London: The Hogarth Press. 18.4 × 12.2 cm. 178 pp. + 6 pp. ads. Light blue cloth, gilt letters on spine.

468. * 11th edition.   1957.

469.   12th edition.   1957. 178 pp. + 5 pp. ads. Blue and white paper covers.

470.   reprint.   1957.

n.d. *C.B.C. BULLETIN No. 4.*
SOME NEW CONCEPTS AND LAWS IN HUMAN BIOLOGY.

471.   1st edition.   n.d. London: Mothers' Clinic. 7 pp.

1934 *C.B.C. BULLETIN No. 5.*
SOME NEW CONCEPTS AND LAWS IN HUMAN BIOLOGY.

472.   1st edition.   1934. London: Mothers' Clinic. 21.5 × 13.8 cm. 8 pp. pamphlet. Title cover.

473. * 2nd edition.

474.   3rd edition.   1948.

1934 *C.B.C. BULLETIN No. 6*
ON SOME ASPECTS OF CONTRACEPTION FOR INDIAN WOMEN.

475. * 1st edition.   1934. London: Mothers' Clinic. 21.5 × 13.8 cm. 8 pp. pamphlet. Title cover.

476. * 2nd edition.   1936.

477.   *   3rd edition.   Feb., 1952.
478.   4th edition.   June, 1952.

[?]   [MARIE STOPES] WOMEN AND IDEALS.
(leaflet)
479.   1st edition.   [?] London: Divorce Reform League.

[?]   [MARIE STOPES] WOMEN, THINK!
(leaflet)
480.   1st edition.   [?] London: Divorce Reform League.

n.d.   *C.B.C. BULLETIN No. 7.*
BIRTH CONTROL FOR WOMEN OUT OF
REACH OF CLINICS.
481.   1st edition.   n.d. London: Mothers' Clinic. 21.5 × 13.8
cm. 4 pp. pamphlet. Title cover.

1934 *CONTRACEPTIVE TECHNIQUE. POST-GRAD-
UATE MEDICAL DEMONSTRATIONS.
482.   1st edition.   1934. London: Mothers' Clinic.
483.   2nd edition.   1935.

1935 MARRIAGE IN MY TIME.
484.   1st edition.   May, 1935. In My Time Series. London:
Rich & Cowan Ltd. 18.3 × 12 cm. 247 pp.
Blue cloth.
485.   variant.   247 pp. + 30 pp. ads. Black cloth, white
letters.
485.a   variant.   224pp. No. ads. Orange cloth, black letters.

1935 *SPACING BABIES FOR HEALTH.
486.   1st edition.   1935. London: Mothers' Clinic. 1 sheet.

1935?*AIMS OF THE CLINIC.
487.   1st edition.   1935. London: Mothers' Clinic. 1p. [there
are several other editions unseen by the com-
piler of this list. No specific data could be
located].

1936 CHANGE OF LIFE IN MEN AND WOMEN.
488.   1st edition.   June 9th, 1936. London: Putnam. 18 × 12
cm. xiv + 282 pp. + 6 pp. ads. Maroon
cloth, gilt letters on spine.
489.   2nd edition.   July, 1938. xiii + 293 pp. + 7 pp. ads. + 5
pp. bib.
490.   reprint.   Nov., 1942.
491.   *   reprint.   Feb., 1944.

492.   3rd edition.   June, 1947, xiv + 293 pp. + 4 pp. ads. + 5 pp. bib.

493.   4th edition.   Jan., 1950.

1939   YOUR BABY'S FIRST YEAR.

494.   1st edition.   Sept., 1939. London: Putnam. 18.4 × 12 cm. ix + 283 pp. Blue cloth, gilt letters.

495.   *   reprint.   Sept., 1942

496.   reprint.   Apr., 1945.

497.   2nd edition.   June, 1949.

1941   BLACK BREEDING. A supplementary indictment to Lord Vansittart's pamphlet *Black Record.* The soul of a people can be changed.

498.   1st edition.   n.d. London: Hutchinson & Co. 18.3 × 10.7 cm. 20 pp. Black and red paper covers.

1942 *TO MAINTAIN BRITISH STRENGTH EVERY BABY SHOULD BE BORN HEALTHY.

499.   1st edition.   1942. London: C.B.C. Society.

1953   THE EVIDENCE OF DR. MARIE C. STOPES TO THE ROYAL COMMISSION ON THE PRESS.

500.   1st edition.   1953. London: the Author. 33 pp.

501. 1956   *C.B.C. BULLETIN No. 8*
PRACTICAL NOTES ON CONTRACEPTIVE TECHNIQUE. London: Mothers' Clinic. 22.4 × 13.8 cm. 8 pp. pamphlet. Title Cover. [1st published in 1951 in *Medical World,* see item 567]

1956   SLEEP.

502.   1st edition.   1956. London: Chatto & Windus. 18.3 × 12 cm. 5 un-numbered leaves + 154 pp. Blue cloth, gilt letters on spine.

503. n.d.   A FEW OF THE THINGS WE HAVE DONE. London: Mothers' Clinic. 20.3 × 12.7 cm. 4 pp.

504. n.d.   LETTER TO THE PEOPLE. London: Mothers' Clinic. 20 × 12.5 cm. 4 pp. Cover title. [signed yours sincerely, Marie Stopes].

505. n.d.   THE MOTHERS' CLINIC. (un-numbered bulletin). London: Mothers' Clinic. 25.5 × 20.5 cm. 3 pp.

506. n.d.   RACIAL OCCLUSIVE CAP. Instructions. How to use the Racial Cap. London: Mothers' Clinic. 1 sheet.

507. n.d.   LEAGUE FOR REMOVAL OF THE TAX ON MARRIAGE. Statement. 26 × 18.2 cm. 1 sheet.

CONTRIBUTIONS TO BOOKS

508. 1920   IMPERIAL AND RACIAL ASPECTS. One chapter in: *The Control of Parenthood,* edited by Sir James Marchant. London and New York: G. P. Putnam's Sons. pp. 190–203.

509. 1920   STATEMENT OF DR. MARIE STOPES. In: *Problems of Population and Parenthood,* Part II, Minutes of Evidence, Monday, March 10, 1919. London: Chapman and Hall Ltd. pp. 242–255.

510. 1930   THE SCIENTIFIC CONSIDERATION OF POPULATION PROBLEMS AND INTERFERENCE WITH THE FREEDOM OF POPULATION. In: Sexual Reform Congress, World League for Sexual Reform. Proceedings of the Third Congress. Edited by Norman Haire. London: Kegan Paul, Trench, Trubner & Co. Ltd. pp. 333–337.

511. 1930   BIRTH CONTROL. In: Sexual Reform Congress, World League for Sexual Reform Proceedings of the Third Congress. Edited by Norman Haire, London: Kegan Paul, Trench, Trubner & Co. Ltd. pp. 105–108.

512. [1950]   One section in: *If I Had My Time Again,* an anthology. Selected by James Marchant. London: Odhams Press. 8 vo. pp. 82–92. Blue cloth.

513. 1953   * Minutes of evidence taken before the Royal Commission on Marriage and Divorce, 32nd day, Thurs., 20th Nov. [including evidence given by M. C. Stopes. pp. [805]–823]. London.

CONTRIBUTIONS TO PERIODICALS

514. 1912   MARRIED WOMEN'S NAMES. How The Law Stands. *The Standard,* April 9.

515. 1913   * INCOME TAX AS A PENALISER OF MARRIAGE. *English Review,* no. 15, August. pp. 146–9.

516. 1919   * SERIES OF ARTICLES in the *Sunday Chronicle.* Including 'The Basis of Truth', 'The Root of Revolution', 'On Beauty', 'On Coffins', 'On Lies'.

517. [1920?]* AN A.1. NATION. 7 pp.

518. [1920]* ASSAULTS ON MARRIAGE [on the enforced resignation of women teachers on marriage].

519. 1922   EARLY DAYS OF BIRTH CONTROL. *The Cambridge Magazine,* Jan. [reprinted. See item 358]

520. 1922   BABIES IN THE RIGHT PLACE. *Women's Pictorial,* March 25.

521. 1922   HOW TO BE IN LOVE THOUGH MARRIED. *Women's Pictorial,* Vol. 3, no. 65. April 1. p. 7.

522. 1922   NOTES FROM THE LAW COURTS. *Birth Control News.* no. 2, June. p. 4., and no. 4, Aug., p. 4.

523. 1922   THE ROOT OF REVOLUTION. *Birth Control News,* no. 6, Oct., p. 3.

524. 1923   THE STOPES CLINIC APPEAL. *Birth Control News,* Vol. III, no. 5.

525. 1923   KNOWLEDGE OF BIRTH CONTROL. *The Arena,* London, Monthly, Vol. 1, no. 1.

526. 1924   BIRTH CONTROL FOR ALL. *John Bull,* Feb. 9.

527. 1924   MY BABY. *Sunday Express,* Apr. 20.

528.   *Birth Control News,* Vol. III, no. 4, Aug. p. 3.

529. 1924 * TEACHING CONTRACEPTION IN MEDICAL SCHOOLS. *Lancet.*

530. 1926   DOMESTIC HEATING. *Nature,* March 6, p. 343.

531. 1926   MY REPLY TO THE ARCHBISHOP. Why I am not 'Mischievous' and 'Harmful'. *The Sunday Chronicle,* Oct. 10. p. 3.

532. 1926   REVIEW: AN IMPORTANT BOOK BY JOHANN FERCH. *Birth Control News,* Vol. V, no. 8. Dec. p. 3.

533. 1927   REVIEW: A GREAT BOOK BY MARY WARE DENNETT. *Birth Control News,* Vol. V, no. 10, Feb. p. 3.

534. 1927   THE BIRTH RATE – LIVING BABIES REDUCE IT. *Birth Control News,* Vol. V, no. 9. p. 3.

535. 1928   MARRIED WOMEN'S NAMES. *The Sackbut,* edited by Ursula Greville. Vol. 8, no. 10. May. pp. 30 2–303.

536. 1930   PROFESSOR McILROY AND THE CAP METHOD. *Birth Control News.* [reprinted in 10,000 Cases. See item 445]

537. 1931   *ZUR GESCHICHTE DER VAGINALEN KONTRAZEPTION. Zentralblatt fur Gynakologie,* no. 343 pp. [reprinted].

538. 1931   COITAL INTERLOCKING. *Clinical Medicine and Surgery,* Vol. 38, no. 3, March. pp. 179–180. [reprinted. See item 447]

539. 1931   SECRET CURES FROM COAL FIRES. *Armchair Science,* Vol. II, no. 12, March. pp. 689–691.

540. 1931   HISTORY AND THEORY OF CONTRACEPTIVE TECHNIQUE. *The Journal of State Medicine,* Vol. 39, no. 6, June. p. 351. [abstract of a lecture delivered at the Royal Institute of Public Health]

541. 1931   PRESENT DAY TECHNIQUE AND CLINICAL RESULTS IN CONTRACEPTION. *The Journal of State Medicine,* Vol. 39, no. 6, June. pp. 352–353.

[abstract of a lecture delivered at the Royal Institute of Public Health].

542. 1931   POSITIVE AND NEGATIVE CONTROL OF CONCEPTION IN ITS VARIOUS TECHNICAL ASPECTS. *The Journal of State Medicine*, Vol. 39, no. 6, June, London monthly. pp. 354–360 [reprinted.]

543. 1931   ONE-CHILD FAMILIES. *The Stork.* London: Putnam. Vol. 2, no. 9. Oct. pp. 4–6.

544. 1931   THE FLIMSY FOUNDATIONS OF THE ANTI CONTRACEPTIONISTS. *Medical Journal and Record*, Vol. 134, no. 10, Nov. 18, 1931. [reprinted].

545. 1931   EARLY VAGINAL CONTRACEPTIVES. *Clinical Medicine and Surgery*, Vol. 38, no. 12, Dec. pp. 889–890.

546. 1931 * SCIENTIFIC BIRTH CONTROL. *Longevity,* Madras: Longevity Book Depot. 8 pp. [reprinted].

547. 1932 * SOME FIGURES ON THE EFFECT OF UTERINE CROWDING BASED ON TEN THOUSAND CLINICAL CASES. Rome: The Comitato Italiano Per lo Studio Dei Problemi Della Popolazione. 6 pp. [Prepared for the International Congress of Studies regarding population problems].

548. 1934   SOME NEW CONCEPTS AND LAWS IN HUMAN BIOLOGY. *Marriage Hygiene*, Kodak House, Bombay, August. pp. 12–15. [reprinted. See items 471, 472]

549. 1934   CONTRACEPTION FOR INDIAN WOMEN. *Marriage Hygiene*, Vol. 1, no. 2, Nov. Bombay: The Times of India Press. pp. 143–145. [reprinted].

550. 1936   ON THE VITAL SOCIAL SIGNIFICANCE OF THE IDEA BEHIND MY NEW TERM 'GEROCEPTION' AS DISTINCT FROM PROCEPTION AND CONTRACEPTION. Bericht. A. Internat. Kongress f. Bevolkerung-swissenschaft, Munchen.

551.   THE CAPTURE OF PROFESSOR McILROY'S CAP. *The Medical Times and Long Island Medical Journal*, Vol. 59, no. 1. 36 pp. [reprinted].

552. 1938   SOME NEW CONCEPTS AND LAWS IN HUMAN BIOLOGY. *Marriage Hygiene*, Aug. 1934. [reprinted as C.B.C. Bulletin no. 4, Mothers' Clinic 1938].

553. 1939   HAVELOCK ELLIS, M.D., *Literary Guide*, Sept. 1 p.

554. 1939   I'M SO TIRED OF WRITING ABOUT THIS. [litter]. *The Daily Mirror*, Aug. 18, p. 14.

555. 1940   CONSTRUCTIVE BIRTH CONTROL. *World Service and Psychic* Review. London: monthly. Vol. 2, no. 3. Jan. p. 64.

556. 1943   AN OPEN LETTER TO THE BISHOP OF ST.

ALBANS. *The Freethinker,* Vol. 63, no. 27. 4th July. pp. 264–265.

557. 1943   EX-MODERNS by S. O. Crates [pseud., i.e. Marie Stopes]. *Poetry Review,* no. 1, 1943.

558. 1943   APPRECIATION from M. C. Stopes. *New Health,* Vol. 18, no. 2. Feb. p. 5.

559. 1945   A REPORT ON POPULATION. *John o'London's weekly,* Oct. 19. p. 29.

560. 1946   COMMENTS BY M.C. STOPES in 'THE HEALTH OF INDIA'. *Journal of the Royal Society of Arts,* Vol. 94, no. 4713. March 15. p. 253.

561. 1948 * RECTAL AND VAGINAL TEMPERATURES. *British Medical Journal,* Vol. 2, July 3rd, London. 2pp. [reprinted].

562. 1949   THE MENACE OF POPULATION. *Courier,* London, monthly. Vol. 13, no. 5. Nov. pp. 80–82.

563. 1949 * GERMAN WOMEN TODAY. *The British Zone Review,* Thurs. Jan. 20th.

564. 1950   SOME NEW CONCEPTS AND LAWS IN HUMAN BIOLOGY. *Japan Planned Parenthood Quarterly,* Vol. 1, no. 2, Apr. – June 1950. p. 47–48. [in Japanese].

565. 1950   THE MOTHERS' CLINIC. *Japan Planned Parenthood Quarterly,* Vol. 1, no. 1. Jan-Mar. 1950. p. 16. [in Japanese].

566. 1951   A MESSAGE FROM DR. MARIE STOPES. *Japan Planned Parenthood Quarterly,* Vol. 2, No. 1–2. Jan-June 1951. p. 9.

567. 1951   PRACTICAL NOTES ON CONTRACEPTIVE TECHNIQUE. *Medical World,* Vol. 75, no. 12, Nov. 23. pp. 317–321. [see item 501].

568. 1952 * THE RECENT PAPAL ANNOUNCEMENT. A Medical Point of View. *The Protestant Standard,* Spring. p. 4.

569. 1953   DONE WITH PASTEURIZATION OF MILK. *Health and You,* March 1953. Vol. 88, no. 1047. pp. 62–64.

570. 1956   SLEEP. *World Digest,* Vol. 35, no. 209, Aug. pp. 65–72.

571. n.d. * 'IS STERILIZATION LEGAL?' *The New Generation,* the magazine of feminists and birth control.

BIRTH CONTROL NEWS

572. 1922   BIRTH   CONTROL   NEWS.   The   Statesmen's
Newspaper. Newspaper format. London: C.B.C. Society.

Monthly:	Vol. I, no. 1, May 1922 –
	Vol. III, no. 12, April 1925.
Quarterly:	Vol. IV, no. 1, June 1925 –
	Vol. IV, no. 4, March 1926.
Monthly:	Vol. IV, no. 5, May 1925 –
	Vol. V, no. 12, April, 1927.
Bi-monthly:	Vol. VI, no. 1, May 1927 –
	Vol. VII, no. 6, March 1929.
Magazine format;	blue covers.
Monthly:	Vol. VIII, no. 1, May 1929 –
	Vol. XVIII, no. 1, June 1940.
War Issues:	Vol. XVIII, no. 2, Dec., 1940.
	Vol. XIX, no. 1, July 1941.
	Vol. XX, no. 1, July 1942.
	Vol. XXI, no. 1, Jan., 1943;
	no. 2, May 1943;
	no. 3, Nov., 1943.
	Vol. XXII, Nov., 1944.
	Vol. XXIII, Nov., 1945.
	Vol. XXIV, Nov., 1946.

Part IV. Literature and Travel

PLAYS AND TRANSLATIONS

1913 PLAYS OF OLD JAPAN; THE NŌ. With translations of the dramas by M.C. Stopes and Professor Joji Sakurai and a Preface by His Excellency Baron Kato, the Japanese Ambassador.

573. 1st edition. 1913. London: Willian Heinemann. 21.5 × 13.7 cm. vii + 102 pp. + 1 p. bib. + 1p. ad., 7 plates. Dark grey boards. [see item] [The Sumida River was produced at Glastonbury Festival School, Aug. 1916].

574. 2nd edition. 1927. Date on title page reads MCXXVII; presumably a mis-print. Facsimile of the first. London: The Eclipse Press. Blue and gold patterned wrappers.

1917 CONQUEST. OR A PIECE OF JADE. A New Play in Three Acts.

575. 1st edition. 1917. N.Y., London: Samuel French. 18.5 × 12.4 cm. 94 pp. × 2 pp. ads. Grey wrappers.

1918 *GOLD IN THE WOOD and THE RACE. Two new plays of life.

576. 1st edition. 1918. London: A. C. Fifield. 17.7 × 11.5 cm. 101 pp. + 2 pp. ads. Rust wrappers.

1923 OUR OSTRICHES. A Play of Modern Life in Three Acts.

577. 1st edition. 1923. London: G. P. Putnam's Sons. 19 × 12.3 cm. 105 pp. + 13 pp. ads. Orange wrappers, ostrich drawing on upper cover. [produced at the Royal Court Theatre, Sloane Sq., 1923].

578. 2nd edition. 1930. 106 pp., no ads. Black cloth, green label on spine. [produced at Royalty Theatre, Dean Street, 1930].

579. 3rd edition. 1939. 18 × 12.4 cm. Orange wrappers.

580. 1923? MARRIED LOVE (later retitled MAISIE'S

MARRIAGE). A story written for the screen by Dr Marie Stopes and Capt. W. Summers [released in various cinemas, 1923].

1925 DON'T TELL TIMOTHY. By Mark Arundel, [pseud., i.e. Marie Stopes].

581.   1st edition.   1925. London: G. P. Putnam's Sons. 20 × 12 cm. 112 pp. Blue paper. [produced at New Scala Theatre, Charlotte St.]

1926 VECTIA – A BANNED PLAY AND A PREFACE ON CENSORSHIP

582.   1st edition.   1926. London: John Ball, Sons & Danielsson, Ltd. 18.3 × 12 cm. 144 pp. Blue cloth. [produced in Sydney, Australia in 1932].

1934 BUCKIE'S BEARS. A Play for Children in six scenes. By Erica Fay [pseud., i.e. Marie Stopes] and Harry Buffkins [pseud., i.e. Harry V. Stopes-Roe].

583.   1st edition.   1934. London: privately printed. 24.5 × 18.2 cm. 75 pp. Blue wrappers. [produced at Royalty Theatre, Christmas 1931–32; Garrick Theatre, 1932–33; Playhouse Theatre, 1933–34 etc.]

584.   Another ed.   Title changed to: THE STORY OF BUCKIE'S BEARS for this and subsequent editions. 1936. London: George G. Harrap & Co. Ltd. 19.5 × 13.3 cm. 124 pp. + 3 pp. ads. Green cloth.

585.   *Another ed.   1946. London: J. Ball, Sons & Danielsson.

POETRY

1914 MAN, OTHER POEMS AND A PREFACE.

586.   1st edition.   1914. London: William Heinemann. 18.3 × 12 cm. xviii + 76 pp. + 2 pp. ads. Blue cloth, gilt letters.

1937 KINGS AND HEROES. By Erica Fay [pseud., i.e. Marie Stopes].

587.   1st edition.   Apr. 1937. London: The Eclipse Press. 18.5 × 12.2 cm. 84 pp. + 1p. ad. Red cloth, yellow letters.

588.   2nd edition.   May 1937. With a preface by Sir Arthur Quiller Couch.

1937 THE CROWNING. A poem.

589.   1st edition.   12th May 1937. The Eclipse Press. 19 ×
13.3 cm. 1 p. sheet. [350,000 printed for
private circulation by the Author].

1939 LOVE SONGS FOR YOUNG LOVERS.

590.   1st edition.   Apr., 1939. London: William Heinemann
Ltd. 21.6 × 14 cm. xi + 70 pp. Orange
cloth, red letters.

591.   Special ed.   1939. 22.5 × 14 cm. Corrected, author
numbered and signed edition. Limited to
150 copies. Hand-made paper. Biscuit paper
covered boards, buckram spine, gilt orna-
ment and letters.

1940 ORIRI.

592.   1st edition.   Sept. 1940. London, Toronto: William
Heinemann Ltd. 18 × 11.5 cm. 27 pp. + 2
pp. ads. Green and silver striped boards.
[N.Y: Putnam's, 1941].

593. n.d.   HYMN FOR AIRMAN. Three verse hymn. Privately
[c.   printed. [Distributed by the Author]. 12.5 × 9 cm. 1
1940] sheet.

1942 INSTEAD OF TEARS. In Memoriam for Officers and
Men who went down with H.M.S. Cossack. 'The Navy is
Here' and especially for Lieut. H. William Rose, R.N.

594.   1st appearance.   Aug. 1942. *Poetry Review*
595.   Limited ed.   3 Dec. 1942. 300 copies. [Little Bookham,
Surrey: Count Potocki of Montalk]. 23 ×
14.5 cm. 7 pp. [un-numbered] Wrappers,
hand-made paper.

596. Cheap paper ed.   1943. 10,000 copies. 17.3 × 12 cm. 12
pp. Grey wrappers, cover title.
In 'Wartime Harvest'. With other poems.
2 editions, 1944 & 1945. [see items 598,
599]

597.   1st separate   1945. London: De La More Press. 19 ×
publication in   12.7 cm. 23 pp. (un-numbered) + 2 pp. ads.
book form.   Blue designed boards.

1944 WARTIME HARVEST. Poems. Preface by The Lord
Alfred Douglas and a letter by George Bernard Shaw.

598.   1st edition.   Nov. 1944. London: Alexander Moring
Ltd. 20.4 × 13 cm. 92 pp. + 2 pp. ads.
Pale green grained boards. [N.Y: Putnams].

| 599. | | 2nd edition. | Nov. 1945. 92 pp. + 3 pp. ads. Green cloth. |

599.   2nd edition.   Nov. 1945. 92 pp. + 3 pp. ads. Green cloth.

1946   THE BATHE.

600.   1st edition.   Oct. 1946. Limited to 500. London: Alexander Moring Ltd. 22.8 × 14.8 cm. 19 pp. + 3 pp. ads. Pastel mottled boards.

WE BURN. Selected Poems of Marie Carmichael Stopes, with portrait frontis and 12 full paper illustrations by Gregorio Prieto.

601.   1st edition.   1949. London: De La More Press, Alex. Moring Ltd. 4to., 27.5 × 21.3 cm. 100 pp. Yellow cloth, red letters.

602.   2nd edition.   1950. 18.5 × 12.3 cm. Orange cloth.

1952   JOY AND VERITY. Other Poems and a Poetic Drama. Prefatory Note by Walter De La Mare.

603.   1st edition.   1952. London: The Hogarth Press. 18.4 × 12 cm. 126 pp. + 2 pp. ads. Orange cloth, gilt letters on spine.

TRAVEL, THE NOVEL AND MISCELLANEOUS

1910   A JOURNAL FROM JAPAN. A Daily Record of Life As Seen By a Scientist.

604.   1st edition.   1910. London, Glasgow: Blackie & Son, Ltd. 21.5 × 14.5 cm. xiv + 280 pp. illus. Cream cloth, brown and orange design and letters.

1919   LOVE LETTERS OF A JAPANESE. Correspondence between Mertyl Meredith, /pseud., i.e. Marie Stopes/, and Kenrio Watanabe, /pseud., Prof. Kenjiro Fujii/, edited by G. N. Mortlake, /pseud., i.e. Marie Stopes/.

605.   1st edition.   1919. London: Stanley Paul & Co. 19.2 × 14 cm. 347 pp. + 4 pp. ads. White cloth, gilt design and letters.

1926   A ROAD TO FAIRYLAND. Fairy Tales. By Erica Fay /pseud., i.e. Marie Stopes/. /Arthur Rackham frontispiece/.

606.   1st edition.   1926. London and N.Y: G. P. Putnam's Sons, Ltd. 20 ×   cm. v + 219 pp. Grey cloth, blue letters.

607.   *Another ed.   1927. xi + 171 pp.

1928   LOVE'S CREATION. By Marie Carmichael, /pseud.,
       i.e. Marie Stopes/.
608.   1st edition.   1928. London: John Bale, Sons &
                Danielsson, Ltd. 19 ×   cm. 416 pp.
                Green, blue and gold patterned paper
                covered boards.
609. 1934 BEDTIME STORY. An interview with Dr Marie
               Stopes. In: *Heads and Tales* by Betty Ross. With an Intro.
               by R. D. Blumenfield. London: Rich & Cowan Ltd.
               1934. pp. 53–63.
610. 1948 A MEMOIR OF THE AUTHOR. Preface to *Poems* by
               Raoul Pugh. London: Macmillan & Co. Ltd. pp. 1–7.
       1949   LORD ALFRED DOUGLAS: HIS POETRY AND
               HIS PERSONALITY.
611.   1st edition.   1949. London: The Richards Press. 18.7 ×
                11.5 cm. 59 pp. + 2 pp. ads. 2 plates.
                Maroon cloth.

CONTRIBUTIONS TO PERIODICALS

612. 1909 A JAPANESE MEDIEVAL DRAMA. (With J.
               Sakurai.) [Article and 'Sumida River', a translation of the
               Japanese Nō, Sumida gawa]. *Transactions of the Royal
               Society of Literature*, 2nd Series, Vol. 29, part III. pp.
               152–178. [reprint. n.d. 26 pp. Cream wrappers].
613. 1915 * SHAKESPEARE AND WAR. *Fortune*, no. 103, June.
               pp. 1057–70.
614. 1916 * IN MEMORY OF SHAKESPEARE. *Fortune*, no. 105,
               May. pp. 830–8.
615. 1916 * CHILDREN'S DAYS IN JAPANESE. *Wheatsheaf*,
               (Birmingham) Mar.
616. 1916 THE PRINCESS. [a fairy tale] *Fortnightly Review.* New
               Series no. 594. June. pp. 1080–1085.
617. 1916 * LILLETTE. [a fairy tale]. *Millgate Magazine.* [later
               published in slightly different form in *English Review*].
618. 1931 THE LITTLE APPLE TREE. By Erica Fay [pseud., i.e.
               Marie Stopes]. *The Sphere*, Nov. 23, pp. 50–52.
619. 1939 * STREAMLINE POETRY. *Life and Letters Today*, Sept.
620. 1940 * MEMORIES OF MAURICE HEWLETT. *John
               o'London's Weekly*, March 8.
621. 1940 THOMAS HARDY CAME TO MY LIGHTHOUSE.
               I Shall Never Forget Series – 6. In: *John o'London's
               Weekly*, Vol. XLIV, no. 1, 133, Dec. 27. page 1, 4¼ cols.
622. 1940 A POETICAL AUTOBIOGRAPHY. *Kingdom Come*,
               Vol. 1, no. 3, Spring. p. 81–82.

623. 1941   THE STONE WALL. A Short Short Story by Keith Carmichael [pseud., i.e. Marie Stopes]. *Kingdom Come*, Vol. 2, no. 3, Spring. p. 88–89.

624. 1945   THE PERSONALITY OF LORD ALFRED DOUGLAS. A Memorial Tribute. *Poetry Review*, Vol. 36, no. 2, May. p. 87–92.

625. 1948   THE POETRY OF LORD ALFRED DOUGLAS. In: *Transactions of the Royal Society of Literature.* pp. 105–123.

626. 1957   WALTER de la Mare: A further note. In: *The Poetry Review*, Vol. 48, no. 2, Apr. – June. p. 98.

627. n.d.   POETRY, REAL AND MODERN. Some Thoughts and Speculations. *English*, the Magazine of the English Association, Vol. 2, no. 12. pp. 375–383. [reprinted, blue wrappers].

Books and Articles about Marie Stopes

post
1912 WOMEN TRAVELLERS IN THE TROPICS by Louise Lederer. *Woman At Home.*

1914 MEN AND WOMEN TODAY – PROFESSOR MARIE C. STOPES. *The World's Work,* Jan., London: William Heinemann. p. 129.

1915 WOMEN OF DREAMS AND DEEDS – DR. MARIE STOPES. by Reginald R. Buckley. *Lady's Pictorial,* June 12.

1922 A Pestilent Crusade [Article attacking Dr. Marie Stopes] in: *The National Champion,* no. 3. June 3.

1922 'The Mischief of Marie Stopes' by the editor, *John Bull,* Vol. 21, no. 827. April 8.

1927 Begbie, Harold. *Marie Stopes. Her mission and her Personality. An Impression.* Aug., 1922. London: G. P. Putnam's Sons. 39 pp.

1934 Brent, Douglas. 'Dr. Marie Stopes'. In: *The Stork.* Vol. 5, no. 18. Sept. pp. 31–33.

1950 MARIE STOPES, THE UNDAUNTED CRUSADER by Norman Phillips. *John Bull,* Aug. 26. pp. 11–12.

1952 Rodner, Joan. 'Dr. Marie Stopes'. In: *Picture Post,* 23 Feb.

1952 DR. MARIE STOPES. *The Illustrated Weekly of India,* Vol. 73, no. 21, May 25.

1955 TRUTH IN SUBSTANCE AND IN FACT. An account of the 'Birth Control' Libel Action: Stopes v. Sutherland and Harding & More, Ltd, with verbatim Reports of the HOUSE OF LORDS JUDGEMENTS. London: Harding & More Ltd (Printed for Private circulation). 89 pp. Blue cloth.

1953 Barttelot, Peter. 'She Put Poetry Into Marriage, Marie Stopes – Modern Crusader'. In: *The Outspan,* June 12. p. 22–25.

1959 Fox, Dr. Adams, Archdeacon of Westminster. 'Marie Stopes' In: *The Poetry Review,* Vol. I, no. 2, April-June 1959. pp. 86–88. [An address delivered at the Memorial Service in St. Martin-in-the Fields, London, 15 Oct. 1958.]

1967   Box, Muriel, editor, 'The Trial of Marie Stopes', London: Femina Books Ltd. 392 pp. photo-frontis.

1973   Stocks, Mary. 'Dr. Marie Stopes', Chapter III of 'Still more Commonplace'. An autobiography. Pub: Peter Davies. pp. 18–29.

1973   Hall, Ruth. 'Sparking the Love Revolution'. Observer Colour Supplement, July 15th.

1974   Stopes-Roe, Harry and Scott, Ian. 'Marie Stopes and Birth Control.' Priory Press. Oct.

INDEX